LIVING IN THE WILD

LEOPARDS

Claire Throp

a Capstone company — publishers for children

Raintree is an imprint of Capstone Global Library Limited, a company incorporated in England and Wales having its registered office at 7 Pilgrim Street, London, EC4V 6LB – Registered company number: 6695582

www.raintreepublishers.co.uk
myorders@raintreepublishers.co.uk

Text © Capstone Global Library Limited 2014
First published in hardback in 2014
Paperback edition first published in 2015
The moral rights of the proprietor have been asserted.

Edited by Clare Lewis and Adrian Vigliano
Designed by Tim Bond
Original illustrations © HL Studios
Picture research by Tracy Cummins
Originated by Capstone Global Library Ltd
Printed and bound in China

ISBN 978 1 406 27344 1 (hardback)
17 16 15 14 13
10 9 8 7 6 5 4 3 2 1

ISBN 978 1 406 27351 9 (paperback)
18 17 16 15
10 9 8 7 6 5 4 3 2 1

A full catalogue record for this book is available from the British Library.

Acknowledgments

The author and publisher are grateful to the following for permission to reproduce copyright material:
Corbis p. 39 (REUTERS/Mike Hutchings); Dreamstime.com p. 9d (© Chris Moncrieff); Flickr p. 9b (Karen Stout); Getty Images pp. 6 (Panoramic Images), 7 (Joseph Van Os), 15 (Martin Harvey), 16 (Anup Shah), 19 (Stuart Westmorland), 22 (Sergey Gorshkov), 25 (DENIS-HUOT / hemis.fr), 26 (Nigel Pavitt), 27 (Don Johnston), 31 (Werner Bollmann), 36 (Joel Sartore), 37 (Dave Hamman), 43 (Minden Pictures/ZSSD), 45 (James Hager); Shutterstock pp. 5, 9a, 29 (Eduard Kyslynskyy), 9c (Howard Klaaste), 9e, 17 (Volodymyr Burdiak), 9f (EcoPrint), 9g (Lilyana Vynogradova), 9h (Graur Razvan), 11 (Karen Givens), 23 (mario.bono), 33 (BlueOrange Studio), 35 (javarman); Superstock pp. 13 (Gerard Lacz Images), 18 (NHPA), 40 (FLPA), 41 (Minden Pictures).

Cover photograph of a leopard reproduced with permission of Getty Images (Danita Delimont).

We would like to thank Michael Bright for his invaluable help in the preparation of this book.

Every effort has been made to contact copyright holders of any material reproduced in this book. Any omissions will be rectified in subsequent printings if notice is given to the publisher.

Disclaimer

Contents

Some words are shown in bold, **like this**. You can find out what they mean by looking in the glossary.

What are big cats?

What's that up in the tree? It's a leopard finding a place to rest in the heat of the day. Leopards are far more active at night when it's cooler. That's when they do most of their hunting.

Mammals

Big cats such as leopards are mammals. Mammals have fur or hair on their body and use lungs to breathe. Most give birth to live young, and mammal babies feed on milk from their mother. Does this description sound familiar? It should – humans are also mammals.

Cats

There are 36 **species** in the cat family, including the **domestic** cat you might have at home! But only a small number are known informally as big cats. One definition of big cats includes all the species of *Panthera*, or roaring cats. Tigers are the largest of the roaring cats, followed by lions, jaguars, and leopards. Some scientists also describe the cheetah, puma, snow leopard, and clouded leopard as big cats.

Cats are great hunters, usually searching for food at night because their vision is often a lot better than that of their prey, and because it's cooler. All their senses are excellent, helped by rotating ears and sensitive vibrissae (whiskers).

LENGTH OF HAIR

The hairs of an Amur leopard's coat change in length from summer to winter. In summer, they are 2.5 centimetres (about 1 inch) long, but in winter they grow to nearly 7 centimetres (3 inches).

Leopards are amazing animals, but many subspecies are struggling to survive in the wild.

What are leopards?

There are thought to be nine subspecies of leopard, each named after where it is found: African, Amur, Arabian, Central Asia (Persian), Indian, Javan, Indo-Chinese, Northern Chinese, and Sri Lankan. A recent study has suggested that two more subspecies exist: the Anatolian leopard in Turkey and the Balochistan leopard in Pakistan and Afghanistan. Clouded leopards are distinct enough to be regarded as separate species, as are snow leopards.

Leopards usually sleep during the day and hunt in the night.

Leopards have large heads with small round ears and whiskers above their mouths.

Features

Most leopards are yellow to light brown with black spots, known as rosettes. There are some leopards that have black coats, but these are not as common. Leopards' legs are short in comparison to their body.

The average height and weight of leopards varies between subspecies and depends in part on the amount and type of **prey** available. Mountain and desert leopards tend to be smaller than leopards living in woodlands or grasslands. Most females tend to grow to 1.7–1.9 metres (5.5–6.25 feet) in length; males measure 1.6–2.3 metres (5.25–7.5 feet). Females typically weigh 17–58 kilograms (37.5–128 pounds), and males are usually 31–65 kilograms (68–143 pounds).

WHAT'S IN A NAME?

The leopard gets its name from the Greek word *leopardus*, which is a mixture of *leon* (lion) and *pardus* (panther).

How are leopards classified?

Classification is the way that humans try to make sense of the world. Grouping living things together by the characteristics that they share allows us to identify them and understand why they live where they do and behave how they do.

Classification groups

In classification, animals are split into various groups. The standard groups are Kingdom, Phylum, Class, Order, Family, Genus, and Species. Sometimes, further classification involves adding more groups such as a subspecies. Each of the standard groups contains fewer and fewer members. For example, there are far more animals to be found in the class Mammalia (mammals), than animals in the family Felidae (cats). Animals are given an internationally recognized two-part Latin name. This helps to avoid confusion if animals are known by different common names in different countries. The leopard's Latin name is *Panthera pardus*, for example.

Evolution of cats

While the first cat-like mammals appeared 60 million years ago, it is thought that the first true cats appeared about 25 million years ago. One was Proailurus, meaning 'early cat', which was an animal the size of a large domestic cat. The family Felidae includes modern wild cats such as leopards and other big cats as well as domestic cats. Members of this family are called felids.

This feline family tree shows estimated dates of when new lines evolved.

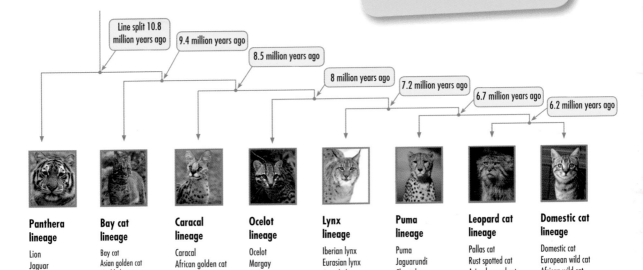

Line split 10.8 million years ago

9.4 million years ago

8.5 million years ago

8 million years ago

7.2 million years ago

6.7 million years ago

6.2 million years ago

Panthera lineage

Lion
Jaguar
Leopard
Tiger
Snow leopard
Clouded leopard

Bay cat lineage

Bay cat
Asian golden cat
Marbled cat

Caracal lineage

Caracal
African golden cat
Serval

Ocelot lineage

Ocelot
Margay
Andean mt. cat
Pampas cat
Geoffroy's cat
Kodkod
Tigrina

Lynx lineage

Iberian lynx
Eurasian lynx
Canada lynx
Bobcat

Puma lineage

Puma
Jaguarundi
Cheetah

Leopard cat lineage

Pallas cat
Rust spotted cat
Asian leopard cat
Fishing cat
Flat-headed cat

Domestic cat lineage

Domestic cat
European wild cat
African wild cat
Chinese desert cat
Desert cat
Black-footed cat
Jungle cat

AMUR LEOPARD

The Amur leopard is the world's most **endangered** cat. In the first successful snow-track census since 2007, between 43 and 45 adult Amur leopards were counted. This is an increase on the previous estimate of 35 leopards.

Classification disagreements

The genus *Panthera* is still being changed and added to today. Scientists disagree over which species are most closely related to each other.

Clouded leopards are a different genus from leopards – *Neofelis* rather than *Panthera* – and have differences in teeth and skull shape. Snow leopards were once thought to be very different from leopards and had their own genus. However, they have now been returned to the *Panthera* genus after it was discovered that they are most closely related to tigers. They are still very different from leopards, though.

There are also issues over the number of subspecies. Some scientists claim there are seven rather than nine, while others suggest 15 subspecies or even more. Changes are suggested as new methods of determining species emerge. Scientists are now using **genetics** to work out differences.

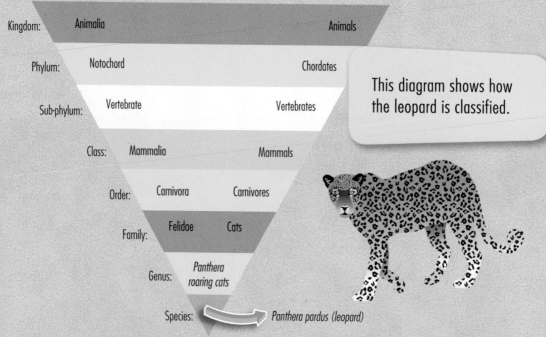

Kingdom:	Animalia	Animals
Phylum:	Notochord	Chordates
Sub-phylum:	Vertebrate	Vertebrates
Class:	Mammalia	Mammals
Order:	Carnivora	Carnivores
Family:	Felidae	Cats
Genus:	*Panthera* roaring cats	
Species:		*Panthera pardus* (leopard)

This diagram shows how the leopard is classified.

Carl Linnaeus included the leopard in his book *Systema Naturae* in 1758. The book introduced the first modern way of classifying animals. This makes the leopard one of the first animals to be named within the modern system of classification.

Believe it or not, both of these big cats are leopards!

Black leopards

Leopards were once thought to be a mixture of lion and jaguar. They were only correctly distinguished from other big cats just over 100 years ago. The confusion existed partly because of the black leopard, which can be born into a family alongside 'normal' yellow leopards. Black leopards are melanistic. A **mutation** in their **genes** causes larger amounts of dark colour in their skin and fur. Black leopards sometimes still have rosettes, but they are not as easy to see!

Where do leopards live?

A habitat is the place where an animal lives. The habitat has to provide everything the animal needs from food to shelter. An animal is dependent on its habitat.

The most common leopard is the African leopard. It mainly lives in sub-Saharan Africa, but it is thought that there might still be small, isolated populations that live in North Africa. The leopard is the last big cat to live in the Atlas Mountains of Morocco. However, there have been no official sightings of leopards in North Africa since 2002. Other small populations can be found in southern Asia, the Middle East, and the Arabian Peninsula. Most Amur leopards live in the Primorskii region of Russia, in **temperate** forests. Their name comes from the Amur region along the Russia-China border. Leopards can be found throughout much of Iran and are particularly common in mountainous areas.

Use this map to see where leopards live around the world.

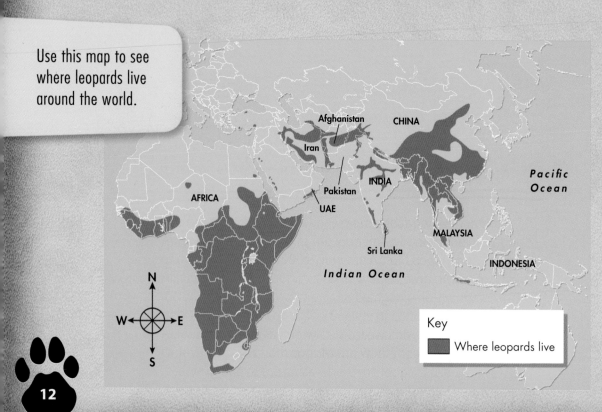

Afghanistan
CHINA
Iran
INDIA
AFRICA
Pakistan
UAE
MALAYSIA
Sri Lanka
Pacific Ocean
INDONESIA
Indian Ocean

N
W E
S

Key

Where leopards live

Habitat

Leopards live in the widest range of habitats of any cat: rainforests, grasslands, mountainous areas, woodlands, and deserts. A leopard has even been seen 5,638 metres (18,497 feet) up on Mount Kilimanjaro in Tanzania. As long as there are plenty of prey animals to hunt and areas in which to take cover, the leopard can survive.

PERSIAN LEOPARDS

It is thought that 65 per cent of wild Persian leopards in Asia live in Iran.

Sri Lankan leopards are often larger than other subspecies of leopard.

What adaptations help leopards survive?

An adaptation is something that allows an animal to live in a particular place in a particular way. Adaptations arise as species **evolve** over thousands of years.

A leopard's body

A leopard's body is adapted to help it hunt. Huge shoulder muscles and powerful front legs help in catching and bringing down large prey. A leopard's shoulder blades have strong muscles attached that help it to climb trees. Their tail is almost as long as their body and helps them to balance as they move through trees.

LEAPS AND BOUNDS

Leopards are capable of leaping 3 metres (10 feet) in the air and to a distance of 6 metres (20 feet).

LISE HANSSEN

Lise Hanssen is a field biologist who has spent many years working in big cat conservation, including helping leopards, lions, and cheetahs, particularly in Namibia. She was the co-founder of the Africat Foundation and was its director for 10 years. She has also developed a system for releasing captive leopards and cheetahs back into the wild.

A leopard has very large paws compared to the size of the rest of its body.

Leopards also have large paws with curved, retractable claws that help them to grab and hold on to prey. Their claws also help them to climb trees. Retractable claws are usually hidden inside the leopard's paw. This helps to keep them sharp and prevents them wearing away as the leopard moves around. When needed, the leopard can choose to pull the claws out.

While most leopards have short legs in comparison to their body, the Amur leopard's legs are longer. This allows it to move through the snow in the Russian forests, where it is often cold and snowy.

A leopard's head

Leopards have very large skulls and this means their jaws are extremely powerful. This allows them to kill and carry animals much larger than themselves. Some leopards can even drag carcasses up trees.

A leopard's tongue has backward facing spines, called papillae, which are used to scrape food off the bones of their prey. The spines are also useful for **grooming** fur.

Leopards have long, sensitive whiskers that help while they are hunting at night. They ensure that the leopard does not bump into things in the dark. The northern Chinese leopard has amazing whiskers that move back when it is sniffing something, move forward to help guide it while walking in the dark, and stick out to the side when the leopard is resting. They also have long hairs in their eyebrows to protect their eyes while they are moving through thick forest.

Grooming is how a leopard keeps itself clean.

WHISKER SPOTS

Whisker spots can help to identify leopards. The patterns are not unique to each animal, though. Between one and five whisker spots can be found on either side of the face above the whiskers. A leopard's spot pattern might be shown like this: 2:1. This would indicate two spots on the left cheek and one on the right.

POACHING

At least four leopards are poached every week in India. This is despite the fact that leopards are a protected species in India and trade in their body parts is banned. A report says that from 2001 to 2010, 2,294 leopards were trafficked in India, mainly to other Asian countries such as China.

A light-reflecting layer of cells in a leopard's eyes, called tapetum lucidum, helps them to see at night.

Senses

Leopards have very good vision. Forward-facing eyes show they are **predators**. This positioning of the eyes allows them to judge distances better, which is useful for hunting.

Their hearing is also excellent, helped by small, round ears that can rotate from side to side, allowing leopards to hear distant sounds from all directions. They can hear five times better than humans can.

UNIQUE PATTERN

A leopard's spots are unique like the human fingerprint, which means they can be used to identify individual leopards.

18

Rosettes

Leopards are well known for being stealthy hunters. Part of the reason they are so good at staying hidden is because the pattern of rosettes, or spots, on their fur helps them to blend into their surroundings. Black melanistic leopards are almost invisible in darker areas of the forest.

The shape of a leopard's rosettes is different depending on where it lives. In South Africa, the rosettes tend to be square, but in East Africa they are circular. Leopards have similar patterns of rosettes on their fur to jaguars. However, the leopard doesn't have a black spot in the middle of its rosettes.

Other spots

White spots on the back of a leopard's ears and on the end of its tail are used to help leopards find each other in long grasses. Female leopards walk with the white tip of their tail pointing up when leading their cubs.

The colour and rosette pattern on a leopard's fur is excellent for camouflage while hunting.

What do leopards eat?

Living things in any habitat depend on each other. This is called interdependence. Animals eat other animals or plants in order to get energy. They in turn may be eaten by bigger animals. These links between animals and plants are called food chains. Many connected food chains add up to a food web.

A food chain starts with a plant because plants are the only organisms that can make their own food. They are called producers. **Consumers** eat plants or other animals. Leopards are consumers and they are called carnivores because they eat meat. Animals that eat other animals are known as predators. The animals they eat are known as prey.

Leopards are opportunistic feeders, which means they can eat anything from birds to reptiles to fish, but usually eat medium to small mammals, such as antelope, gazelles, and warthogs. In Africa, leopards eat baboons. When they live near human populations, leopards often eat **livestock**, dogs, and occasionally people. Leopards are near the top of the food web but can be attacked by other carnivores.

BEVERLY AND DERECK JOUBERT

Beverly and Dereck Joubert have spent 25 years using their wildlife films and photographs to help support conservation of big cats and other species in Africa. They have made 22 films, produced 10 books, and written a number of scientific articles. The couple work for National Geographic as Explorers-in-residence, and are the founders of the Big Cat Initiative, which aims to highlight the problems faced by big cats in the wild as well as provide funding for conservation projects.

Leopard

Hawk

Baboon

Scorpion

Impala

Seed-eating bird

Locust

Grass

This food web shows how energy flows from one organism to the next.

Scavenging and storing

Leopards do sometimes **scavenge** if prey is hard to find. They might steal food from cheetahs or a hyena if it is on its own. Lions and hyenas have been known to steal leopards' food too.

Leopards are also likely to store food for later. Some leopards keep carcasses in trees to come back to but most cover their kill in soil and leaves to keep it hidden. Even while having this store of food, leopards may continue to hunt.

Drinking

Leopards are facultative drinkers, which means they don't have to actually drink very often. This is because most of their water comes from the prey they eat.

Even though leopards do not have to drink every day, if there is water available they often drink after eating.

A swift bite to the throat is enough to kill many of the leopard's prey animals.

LEOPARD CONSERVATION SCIENCE PROJECT

The African Wildlife Foundation set up the Leopard Conservation Science Project at Kruger National Park in South Africa in 2010. It was in response to the fact that little is known about the conservation status of leopards. One of their main aims is to get a good estimate of leopard numbers. To do this, they have placed camera traps in specific areas of the park to capture images of wildlife movement. They also plan to use GPS collars to track leopards. The results will be used to provide advice on conservation practices, particularly with regard to human-leopard conflict.

What is a leopard's life cycle?

The life cycle of an animal covers its birth to its death and all the different stages in between. A leopard's life cycle includes birth, juvenile, and adulthood. During adulthood they **reproduce** and have young.

Mating

Females have a seven-day period every six or seven weeks when they can become pregnant. When they are ready to mate, females rub their scent onto trees and call loudly. Male leopards will travel long distances for the opportunity to mate. The couple will usually stay together for a few days before separating again.

Pregnancy and birth

Leopards are pregnant for 96 days on average. They can give birth at any time of year, but peak time for giving birth is often during the rainy season. This is because there is likely to be more food available at this time. In Siberia and China, leopards tend to breed in January and February. There are usually two to three cubs born in a litter, but there can be up to six.

Cubs

Cubs are very small when first born and are blind and helpless, so they are hidden by their mother for about 8 weeks until they are big enough to join her. They are usually hidden in dense bushes or hollow tree trunks for up to 36 hours while the mother is hunting. The mothers move the hiding place frequently to avoid detection by predators such as lions. Cubs are suckled for about 3 months, but are fed meat from 6–7 weeks old.

Leopard cubs weigh 0.5 kilograms (about 1 pound) when they are first born. This female is carrying a one-month-old cub.

Young leopards

Mothers teach their offspring how to hunt and survive. After three months, cubs may even join their mother on hunts. Cubs have all the skills they need to look after themselves by the age of about 10 months. They are usually fully independent by the age of 20 months but can stay with their mother for up to two years. While males tend to move further away from their mother's **territory** when they leave her care, females may well have overlapping territory with her.

The cycle begins again

Leopards have babies every 15–24 months from an average of 2.5 years old until they're about 8.5. Wild leopards can live to the age of 10–12, although the oldest known leopard reached the age of 17. In captivity, leopards can live longer – up to 23 years.

After they leave their mother's territory, male leopards usually live alone.

Black leopards, like this one, are often called black panthers, but so are black jaguars. Tigers can also be black, but they are very rare.

REPRODUCTION

One recent study used sightings and photos from eco-tourism lodges in the Sabi Sand Game **Reserve** in South Africa to research the reproductive history of 44 leopards in the area over a period of 32 years. Among other things, they discovered that survival rates of cubs decreased as the mother got older and that males were responsible for 40 per cent of cub deaths.

How do leopards behave?

Leopard behaviour differs depending on where they live, but there are a few things that are common for all leopards. They are more wide-ranging and **adaptable** than other big cats.

Territory

Leopards mark their territory with claw marks on trees, urine, and faeces. They also use loud rasping coughs to make sure other leopards know the boundaries of their territory. They usually know roughly where other leopards are. Territory held by males is usually larger than that of females and it may overlap several females' territory. On average a male's home range is 35 square kilometres (13.5 square miles) and females have 13 square kilometres (5 square miles). Leopards have a larger territory if their habitat is a very dry one. Leopards tend not to stay in one place for more than a few days.

Do leopards kill humans?

Leopards don't often kill humans, but it is becoming more frequent as humans move further into leopard territory. Sometimes if a leopard is ill, it may kill a human because humans are easy prey. However, one leopard regularly killed humans – between 1918 and 1926 it killed 125 people in villages in the foothills of the Himalayas. It became known as the 'the man-eating leopard of Rudraprayag'.

This leopard is sniffing the scent marks that have been left on the tree.

ARABIAN LEOPARD

Arabian leopards are listed as critically endangered on the IUCN red list, which means there are fewer than 250 left in the wild. They are thought to be found only on the Arabian Peninsula, and are probably **extinct** in the wild in several countries, including Jordan and United Arab Emirates. Some leopards have been taken into captive breeding programmes, headed by the Breeding Center for Endangered Arabian Wildlife in the

Nocturnal and solitary

Leopards are mainly **nocturnal** and spend their days resting or sleeping. They usually become more active when it gets dark until just after the sun rises. They are generally **solitary** animals, only coming together for a short time to mate. If they meet apart from that, there can often be fights.

Feeding behaviour

In some countries, leopards eat smaller prey because other carnivores may be more dominant. In India, for example, tigers tend to dominate the centre of a national park, where there are plenty of deer to eat, while the leopard is forced to live at the edges.

DR GEORGE SCHALLER (BORN 1933)

Dr George Schaller is known as one of the founding fathers of wildlife conservation. He is now vice president of Panthera (a wild cat conservation group) and senior **conservationist** at the Wildlife Conservation Society. His focus is on snow leopards.

AMUR LEOPARD AND TIGER ALLIANCE

The Amur leopard is ten times more endangered than the Amur tiger. Zoos brought the leopard's plight to the attention of the public in the 1990s. Now the Amur Leopard and Tiger Alliance (ALTA) has set up a conservation programme for them, including habitat protection and compensation schemes for deer farmers. The Zoological Society of London is a member of ALTA. ZSL in partnership with Moscow Zoo plan to reintroduce captive leopards from zoos to the wild. Their aim is to set up a reserve in one of the areas where the leopard used to live, north of Vladivostok in Russia.

Leopards can swim and sometimes hunt in the water, eating fish and crabs. They also like to play in water!

A DAY IN THE LIFE OF A LEOPARD

A leopard's day is made up of hunting, feeding, playing, and lots of sleeping!

Hunting and feeding

When leopards are stalking prey, they make sure they get as close as 3–10 metres (1–33 feet) before they attack. They know they will not normally be able to outrun most prey.

The fact that leopards eat a variety of food means that even if their preferred prey is not available, they can survive by hunting other animals. If a leopard manages to catch quite a large prey animal, such as an adult antelope, the **carcass** can last for two weeks. Most of the time, though, a leopard has to hunt every few days. A female that has cubs will normally have to hunt twice as often as other leopards in order to get enough food to feed her young.

Playing

Cubs in particular enjoy playing. Play is very important for learning new skills. **Stalking** – creeping along slowly while hidden in long grasses or other cover – is one playtime activity. Pouncing – jumping on something with claws out – is another, especially if you can pounce on your brothers and sisters! The other part of hunting is chasing and that's even more fun!

Leopards can sleep for up to 20 hours a day.

Sleeping

By far the largest part of the day is spent sleeping. Leopards often like to sleep in trees but can rest in caves or thick vegetation. Occasionally they can be seen sunbathing!

How intelligent are leopards?

Intelligence is difficult to measure in animals. It usually refers to how animals hunt and communicate with each other.

Excellent hunters

Leopards are cunning hunters and possibly the stealthiest big cats. They are ambush hunters, which means they like to stalk their prey first. Then they pounce on it before the prey has a chance to escape. They sometimes drop onto prey from the branches of trees. Leopards are well camouflaged in trees. After catching prey, leopards bite the back of the animal's neck to paralyse it and then use their powerful jaws to strangle the animal.

Communication

Leopards are usually silent, but they can growl and spit if really angry. They can cough to warn other leopards to keep away and they can purr when they are content or eating.

SIGNALS

Leopards flip their tails over to show the white underside if they are not hunting. Herds of antelope will call loudly to each other as a warning but will not mob the solitary leopard. The antelope appear to be letting the leopard know they have seen it, while the leopard knows that it has been seen. It seems to be a signal aimed at conserving energy, so both antelope and leopard realize that a hunt is not possible.

Leopards know that if there are lions or other predators around they will probably lose their kill unless they drag it up a tree. This is called hoisting. The carcass is usually left on the ground if there are no predators near by.

DR QUINTON MARTINS

Quinton Martins is a South African conservationist who co-founded the Cape Leopard Trust in 2004. He was a safari guide in Botswana and the Sabi Sand Reserve in South Africa. He saw many leopard tracks but never an actual leopard. Very little research had been done on leopards – partly because they are so difficult to find in the wild – and this inspired Martins to study leopards and try to make a difference.

What threats do leopards face?

Habitat loss

One of the main problems for leopards is loss of habitat. A constant growth in the human population means land that leopards once roamed is now being transformed into homes, farms, and ranches for people. Leopards like to spend a lot of time in trees, but many of these have been chopped down for building or for land clearance. Of course, it is not just leopards that are affected but also their prey.

Inbreeding

Fragmentation of land means that only small pockets of leopard habitat remain in some areas. This can lead to further problems such as inbreeding, as male leopards find it difficult to get from one area to another. Inbreeding is where many generations of leopards are bred from the same small group.

This rare Amur leopard is being held in captivity in the United States.

Hunting

Leopards are one of the 'big five' wild animals that tourists like to see when on safari. The term 'big five' comes from the time they were one of the five most popular animals to shoot. Nowadays, 'trophy hunting' continues. Leopard skin rugs, coats from leopards' fur, and other such trophies are desired by some people. This trade is illegal but still goes on in secret on the **black market**.

Canned hunting is a legal practice where leopards are bred specifically for hunting. They are often kept in enclosed areas (with electric fencing) so that they cannot escape from the hunters.

The trade of leopard skins is a problem in many parts of the world, including Botswana.

LOSS OF RANGE

Leopards have lost more than 50 per cent of their historic range in Asia and nearly 40 per cent in Africa. It is thought that between 1970 and 1983, 80 per cent of the Amur leopard's habitat was lost due to logging, forest fires, and humans turning land into farms.

Killed by people

Leopards are frequently killed by farmers – either poisoned or shot – after the leopards have attacked their livestock. This happens more often nowadays because humans are encroaching on leopard ranges. The Amur leopard preys on deer, and when wild deer are not available, they are likely to attack deer farmed for their antlers, which are used in Asian medicine. Owners of deer farms retaliate by killing any leopards preying on their stock. This is probably the most serious current threat to Amur leopards.

Poaching

It is illegal to poach leopards for body parts in South Africa, and those who wish to wear leopard fur as part of a tradition, such as Zulu warriors, have to have a permit from the government. Unfortunately, many African communities are not aware of the problems faced by leopards in the wild and the poaching continues.

In Asia, leopard whiskers are used in some medicines, so leopards are in danger from poachers. Leopard bones are sometimes used as a replacement for tiger bones in Asian medicine.

FAKE LEOPARD SKIN

Tristan Dickerson is a conservationist who discovered that thousands of leopard skins are being used as clothing by members of the Nazareth Baptist Church in southern Africa. Dickerson is trying to get a synthetic (human-made) alternative produced that the church members will be happy to wear. The leader of the church said he had no idea leopards were a threatened species and that he would be willing to allow church members to wear fake fur if the quality was good enough. Some members of the church feel that the fake fur is still too expensive. Others think that wearing it would weaken their religion. So far, Dickerson's fake fur samples have not been approved by the church. He hopes to persuade the church leader to wear the fake fur in order to encourage others to do so too.

These Nazareth Baptist Church members are wearing clothes made out of leopard skins.

How can people help leopards?

Some leopard subspecies are in danger of dying out and a big part of the problem is humans. However, people can also help to protect leopards and their habitats.

Conservation organizations

Conservation organizations help not just by raising money but also in practical ways. Improving public knowledge and understanding about leopards is an important part of what conservation groups do. Conservationists encourage local people to want to protect their local wildlife and their habitats. Research into how leopards live will make it easier for conservationists to come up with plans to help these animals survive.

Eco-tourism

Eco-tourism can be used to help leopards by providing an alternative source of income for local people. Many tourists are interested in seeing animals in the wild but often need a guide to show them where to go and how to behave around the animals. Local people can do this job and other jobs linked to tourism.

Radio-tracking collars allow conservationists to see where leopards go. This will help in planning how to protect the species.

Eco-tourism is important because it brings money into the local economy.

Land purchase

Breeding big cats in captivity and then reintroducing them to the wild is one method of conservation. However, it costs about £30,000 to release a cat back into the wild with only a 15 per cent chance of it surviving and reproducing. Some conservationists now believe that purchasing natural habitat is a better option. This alternative conserves the habitat for all the wildlife and plants that live there.

What can you do?

If you want to help save leopards, there are many things you can do. You could donate some pocket money, join a conservation group, such as WWF, or even sponsor a leopard. Telling family and friends what you have read about in this book and on the internet will help – the more people who care about the fate of leopards, the more likely a change can be made.

What does the future hold for leopards?

While leopards are still fairly wide-ranging, five out of the nine subspecies are considered endangered or critically endangered. The leopard's adaptability has helped them as humans have destroyed more and more of their habitat, and captured or killed them for sport, the pet trade, fur, medicine, and to protect livestock.

Most leopards actually live outside protected areas such as national parks. This is one of the main reasons why they are the most persecuted cat. Conservation groups are constantly trying to protect the leopard, but conflicts with humans are on the rise. As the human population continues to increase, more conflicts are likely.

It is important that we don't allow leopards to die out. The more young people – like you – who get involved, the better. Every little bit helps.

CONSERVATION SUCCESS

The Munyawana Leopard Project has been run by conservation organization Panthera since 2002. Results led to changes in hunting laws in northern KwaZulu-Natal, South Africa. Proposals included lowering the number of leopards that could be hunted and making sure that hunts were spread out so that one leopard population was not targeted more than another. Panthera also suggested that the hunting of female leopards and cubs should be banned. These proposals were put into practice in 2006; just two years later, the results could be seen. Populations increased and life for females trying to raise their cubs became more stable. Leopards were also found to be living longer.

Leopards deserve their place
in the natural world.

Leopard profile

Species:	Leopard
Latin name:	*Panthera pardus*
Length:	Females grow to 1.7–1.9 metres (5.5–6.25 feet); males grow to 1.6–2.3 metres (5.25–7.5 feet)
Weight:	Females weigh 17–58 kilograms (37.5–128 pounds); males weigh 31–65 kilograms (68–143 pounds)
Habitat:	Rainforests, grasslands, mountainous areas, woodlands, and desert
Diet:	Mainly medium to small mammals such as small antelope, gazelles, and warthogs. However, leopards eat a wide range of food, including fish, birds, and reptiles.
Number of cubs per litter:	Leopards usually give birth to two to three cubs every 15–24 months. Pregnancy lasts about 3 months.
Life expectancy:	10–12 years. The oldest known leopard was 17.

The rosettes on the coat help camouflage the leopard when hunting.

Large shoulder muscles are useful for bringing down large prey.

Leopards have excellent hearing and eyesight.

Sensitive whiskers help the leopard feel its way at night.

The white tip on the tail helps leopards find each other in long grass.

Strong legs and large paws can hold onto large prey.

Powerful jaws can kill and carry large animals.

Glossary

adaptable able to change to suit conditions and surroundings

black market illegal trade in goods, such as animal body parts

carcass dead body of an animal

conservationist someone who helps to protect animals, plants, and habitats

consumer organism that consumes (eats) plants or animals

domestic tame and kept by people

eco-tourism form of tourism where people go to see wildlife and help to protect nature

endangered when a plant or animal is in danger of dying out

evolve change over time

extinct no longer existing

gene unit that makes up the characteristics of a living thing that are passed from parent to offspring. For example, one particular gene is responsible for eye colour.

genetics study of characteristics passed from parent to offspring

groom clean the fur and skin

livestock farm animals

mutation change in the structure of a gene

nocturnal active at night

predator animal that hunts and eats other animals

prey animal that is hunted and eaten by another animal

reproduce to have offspring

reserve area of protected land set aside for wild animals

scavenge feed on dead animals that have been killed by another predator

solitary alone

species group of organisms that are similar and are able to produce offspring together

stalk to hunt by creeping along quietly and secretly

temperate area that has mild temperatures

territory area of land that an animal views as its own

Find out more

Books

Big Cats, Jonathan Shiekh-Miller (Usborne, 2008)

Face to Face with Leopards, Beverly and Dereck Joubert (National Geographic, 2010)

Leopards (Endangered!), Carol Ellis (Marshall Cavendish Children's Books, 2010)

Websites

www.animals.nationalgeographic.co.uk/animals/mammals/leopard
Learn more about leopards here.

www.bbc.co.uk/nature/life/Leopard
This BBC website has information and some great videos to watch about leopards.

Organizations

Panthera
www.panthera.org
Panthera is a conservation organization that works to protect big cats such as leopards.

WWF
www.wwf.org.uk
WWF works to protect animals and nature and needs your help!
Take a look at their website and see what you can do.

Index